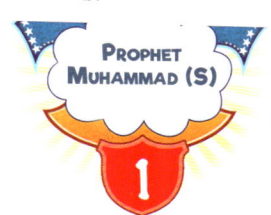

Heavenly Children
The Little General

PROPHET MUHAMMAD (S)
1

Kisa Kids Publications

Dedication

This book is dedicated to the beloved Imām of our time (AJ). May Allāh (swt) hasten his reappearance and help us to become his true companions.

Acknowledgements

Prophet Muḥammad (s): The pen of a writer is mightier than the blood of a martyr.

True reward lies with Allāh, but we would like to sincerely thank the efforts of Shaykh Salim Yusufali, Brother Aliakbar Shaheidari, Sisters Sabika Mithani, Fatemah Mithani, Amna Hussain, Asieh Zarghami, Zahra Sabur, Sajeda Merchant, Kisae Nazar, Sarah Assaf, Nadia Dossani, Fathema Abidi, Fatemeh Eslami, Fatima Hussain, Fatemah Meghji, Sukaena Kalyan, and Zehra Abbas. We would especially like to thank Nainava Publications for their contributions. May Allāh bless them in this world and the next.

Preface

Prophet Muḥammad (s): Nurture and raise your children in the best way. Raise them with the love of the Prophets and the Ahlul Bayt (a).

Literature is an influential form of media that often shapes the thoughts and views of an entire generation. Therefore, in order to establish an Islāmic foundation for the future generations, there is a dire need for compelling Islāmic literature. Over the past several years, this need has become increasingly prevalent throughout Islāmic centers and schools everywhere. Due to the growing dissonance between parents, children, society, and the teachings of Islām and the Ahlul Bayt (a), this need has become even more pressing. Al-Kisa Foundation, along with its subsidiary, Kisa Kids Publications, was conceived in an effort to help bridge this gap with the guidance of ʿulamah and the help of educators. We would like to make this a communal effort and platform. Therefore, we sincerely welcome constructive feedback and help in any capacity.

The goal of the *Heavenly Children* series is to foster the love of Ahlul Bayt (a) in children and to help them establish the 14 Maʿṣūmīn as their role models. We hope that you and your children enjoy these books and use them as a means to achieve this goal, inshāʾAllāh.

We pray to Allāh to give us the strength and *tawfīq* to perform our duties and responsibilities.

With Duʾās,
Nabi R. Mir (Abidi)

Disclaimer: Religious texts have ***not*** been translated verbatim so as to meet the developmental and comprehension needs of children.

Copyright © 2016; 2019 by Al-Kisa Foundation; SABA Global

All rights reserved. First edition 2016. Second edition 2019. No part of this publication may be reproduced, distributed or transmitted in any form or by any means, including photocopying, recording, or other electronic or mechanical methods, without the prior written permission of the publisher, except in the case of brief quotations embodied in critical reviews and certain other noncommercial uses permitted by copyright law. For permission requests, please write to the publisher at the address below.

Kisa Kids Publications
4415 Fortran Court
San Jose, CA 95134
(260) KISA-KID [547-2543]

One day, Ahmad's Baba and Mama shared some exciting news with him.

"Ahmad, guess what! We are going on a very special trip, InshaAllah!" Baba said.

"Yes," Mama said, "we are going to visit the fourteen Ma'soomeen!"

"The fourteen Ma'soomeen?" Ahmad asked. "Can you remind me who they are?"

"The fourteen Ma'soomeen are our role models. They are Prophet Muhammad (s), Sayyidah Fatimah (a), and the twelve Imams (a)!" Mama said.

"But how are we going to visit them?" asked Ahmad. "Didn't Prophet Muhammad (s) die?"

"We visit them by going to the places they are buried," replied Baba. "Prophet Muhammad (s) is buried in the city of Medina."

"Was he born there, too?" asked Ahmad.

"No, he was born in the city of Mecca on the 17th of Rabi ul-Awwal, during the year of the elephant."

"What's the year of the elephant?" asked Ahmad.

"During the year he was born, an evil man named Abraha wanted to destroy the Ka'bah. He marched towards Mecca along with an army of elephants to ruin the Ka'bah, but before he was able to do so, Allah sent birds to drop pebbles on the elephants, stopping them from destroying the Ka'bah!"

"Woah!" Ahmad was amazed. An evil man stopped by a flock of birds! He thought that was incredible. "Tell me more about Prophet Muhammad (s)!" he said.

Mama told him, "Prophet Muhammad's mother's name was Aminah. She was a great woman. His father, Abdullah, passed away before he was born. For the first five years of his life, he was raised by a nurse named Halima. He was then returned to his mother, but she passed away when he was only six years old. His grandfather, Abdul Muttalib, took care of him for some time. After his grandfather passed away, his uncle, Abu Talib, and his uncle's wife, Fatimah bint* Asad, took care of him. They were just like his parents! Do you want to hear a story about Prophet Muhammad (s) from his childhood?"

"Yes!" Ahmad replied eagerly, "Please tell me!"

*Daughter of

1

The hot sun shone brightly through the window as Fatimah bint Asad finished her morning tasks. She looked out the window and admired the tall palm trees filled with clusters of delicious dates. However, one date tree caught her eye — it was an old tree that had become dry and shriveled up. No juicy dates hung from its worn branches.

Suddenly, laughter from the yard caught her attention. She looked over at the children playing.

Little Muhammad (s) shouted, "March!" and all the other children answered, "Yes, sir!"

Every time he gave a command, the kids would cheerfully follow along. Just then, she heard Muhammad (s) tell his friends, "Wait, my dear soldiers, let me run inside and get some water!"

3

4

As Muhammad (s) entered, Fatimah bint Asad could see he was very excited. She gave him a loving kiss on the forehead as he asked, "Mother, may I please have some water? My soldiers are thirsty!" He was always very polite.

Fatimah replied playfully, "Yes, sir! Right away!"

This made Muhammad (s) giggle. He said, "You're my mom! You can't be my soldier!"

Fatimah bint Asad poured some water into a bowl and said, "If I cannot be your soldier, I can at least be your supporter, right?"

Muhammad (s) looked at his mother as he took the water and smiled.

"My supporter? Yes, that's a great idea!" They both laughed heartily.

7

Muhammad (s) picked up his wooden sword and the water. Just like a real, brave general, he declared, "I must go outside and help my soldiers get ready to protect the truth!"

As he ran out the door, he struck the dry date tree in the yard. Fatimah's eyes widened as the dry date tree suddenly began turning green, and big, luscious dates began to fill its branches!

9

Fatimah quickly walked towards the date tree and picked a date from it. She looked at it in wonder and tasted the date. Her eyes lit up! What a delicious date! It was better than any date she had ever tasted!

This wasn't the first time she had witnessed a miracle from Muhammad (s). Every time it was a wonderful surprise. She knew there was something very special about this boy. Being around him always strengthened her belief in Allah and gave her energy!

As she looked at the tree, she remembered how Muhammad (s) had lost his real mother at the young age of six. She thought to herself, *I'm so blessed to raise Muhammad (s) in my home!* Even though she had children of her own, Muhammad (s) was extra special. His foster mother, Halima, had also told Fatimah bint Asad about all the wonderful blessings and miracles that Muhammad (s) had brought to her home, even as an infant.

11

In fact, Halima had shared her own miracle story about a date tree. Halima had told her, "One day, I was passing through the desert with Muhammad (s) and stopped to feed him under a dry date tree. As I finished feeding him, we both fell asleep. When I woke up, I looked up and saw the most amazing sight! The tree behind us had become green again and was full of dates!"

13

14

Another time, Halima was outside with Muhammad (s), tending to the sheep, when one of the baby sheep fell and broke its leg. Muhammad (s) carefully walked over and gently touched the sheep's leg. She was shocked to see the leg instantly heal right before her eyes!

Suddenly, Muhammad (s) walked back inside and started calling out, "Mother! Mother!"

Fatimah turned towards him and hugged him lovingly as she said, "May my father and mother be sacrificed for you*, my son. How can I help you?"

Muhammad (s) replied, "My dearest mother, my soldiers need more energy. Can you please give me some dates so that I may feed my hungry soldiers?"

Fatimah's eyes filled with tears as she kissed Muhammad's (s) divine head and held him tighter.

She replied, "Yes, sir!" and then quickly grabbed a basket and filled it with dates from the very tree Muhammad (s) had just brought back to life.

*In our ahadith and du'as, when someone wants to show the highest level of loyalty and love towards another person, they use this expression.

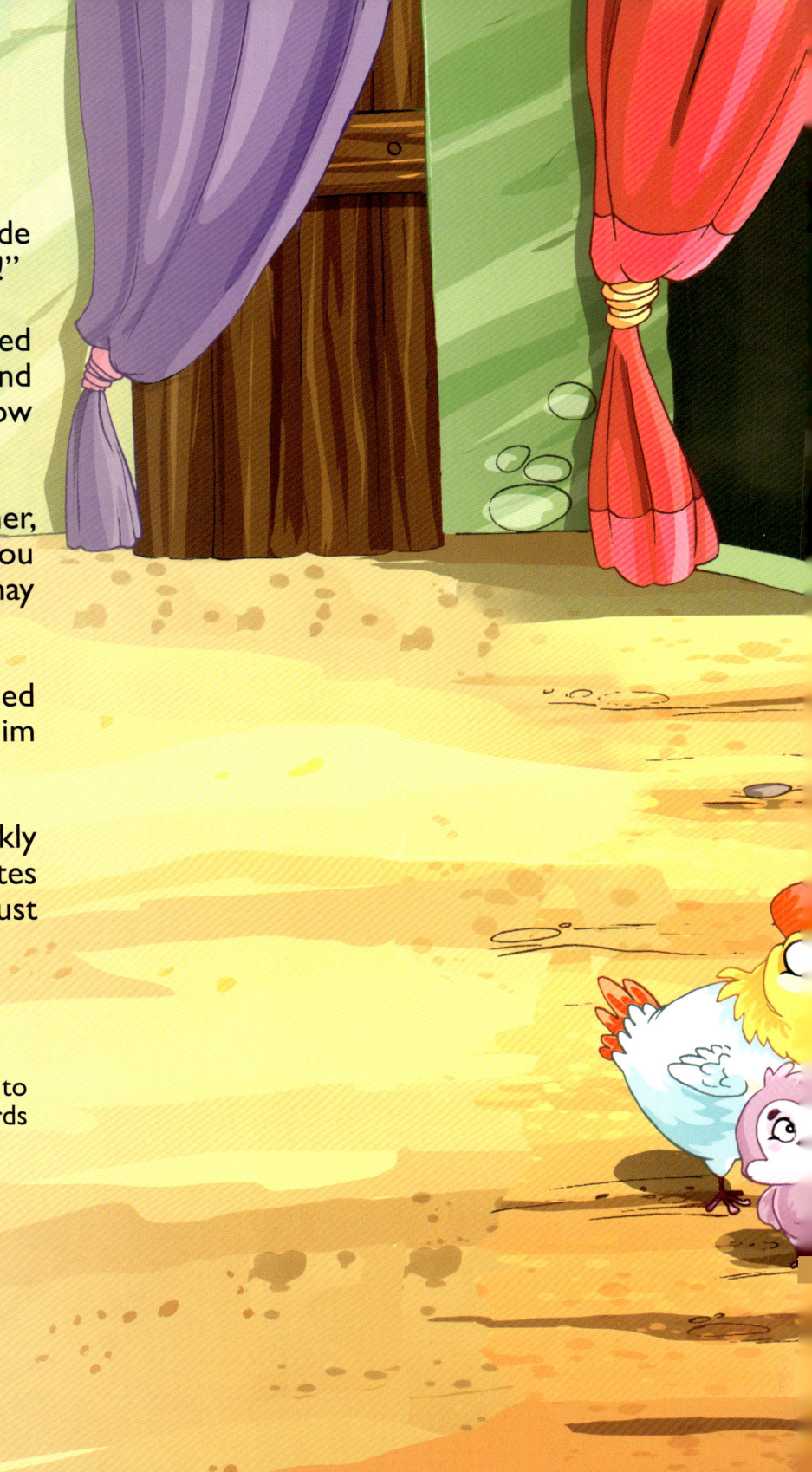

17

Fatimah followed Muhammad (s) as he ran outside to his friends and handed out the dates. She raised her hands up and, filled with emotion, asked Allah to bless her with a child who could be Muhammad's assistant and supporter in his divine purpose. We know her du'a was answered many years later, when she gave birth to Imam Ali (a), who became Prophet Muhammad's loyal partner, supporter, and successor!

As Fatimah looked out at the children, she smiled contentedly and quietly walked back inside. Before entering the house, she turned back to look at the renewed date tree one more time. It seemed to outshine all the other trees, almost as if it felt honored at the very touch of young Muhammad (s).

Biḥār ul-Anwār, Vol. 15, P. 340